That's Sick!

NATIONAL LAMPOON'S
Rudest and Crudest Cartoons

CB
CONTEMPORARY
BOOKS

CHICAGO

That's Sick!

Cartoons By:

M. K. Brown

John Caldwell

Callahan

Thomas W. Cheney

Cotham

Leo Cullum

Bud Grace

Sam Gross

John Jonik

Mankoff

Howard Margulies

Revilo

Charles Rodrigues

P. Steiner

Ed Subitzky

Larry Trepel

M. Twohy

P. C. Vey

Jack Ziegler

"Hey, want to see some sewage?"

Bob the Frog

"Romulus is going to found Rome and Remus is going to become a pimp."

"Gesundheit!"

"... And then we have the 'Terrorist Special' where you're shot in the head and then dumped at the airport of your choice."

*"Since you have assured me that fantasies
are quite normal, Doctor, I'll describe one
in particular that gives me immense pleasure.
My husband is lying in bed nude while a beautiful
young girl is squatting just above his face. He slowly
raises his head to her pubic area, and
I hit them both with a flamethrower!"*

"Well, I hope you're satisfied. Now you've scared the others away."

"*Shall I wait up for you?*"

"Let me through! I'm an upholsterer!"

"Just as I thought. This mummy has a 'curse'!"

"My brother Bruce wants to know if you would
blow him instead of the house."

"Chief, I don't like to tell you how to run your department, but it's an election year and the unions are raising hell with me, so from now on, when electrodes are applied to prisoners' genitals, it's gotta be done by union electricians only!"

"How many times have
I told you not to leave crumbs in the bed?"

"I'm sorry, sir, but I've got to ask you another question. I heard someone in the courtroom shout out the correct answer."

"No one's been sleeping in my bed, but my tennis
racket smells like tuna fish!"

"We thought a nice little birdie would cheer you up."

"Oh, come on! I didn't put that much poison in!"

PCVEY

"MY WIFE AND MY BEST FRIEND.
HOW COULD I HAVE BEEN SO BLIND?"

"Well and good, gentlemen. But do you think the enemy will be
using such tiny ships?"

"Today I am a man!"

"If I were you I'd go to the country for a while... but then I have a half-million-dollar estate with two swimming pools and three tennis courts to go to and you don't, so maybe you'd better stay home."

"Excuse me for interrupting, madam, but before you go on allow me to make these comments: one, I have no desire for you to do my cooking; two, I neither want nor need you to pay my rent; three, I'm very sorry you cried the whole night long; and four, and perhaps most important, I think you've called the wrong Bill Bailey."

"Mister, want these rubbers?"

"In a minute! In a minute!"

"*Damn it! I just stepped in wolf shit!*"

"Darling, we can't go on meeting like this. My husband is starting to get suspicious."

"So far so good, but now what are we going to do
about the burglar alarm in my vagina?"

"You should have phoned, Mr. Broughton—
Glenda's not here this week. She's working skid row
while she has her period."

"Boy! That was either the best head or the best ass I've ever had!"

"Well, how was I supposed to know you were saving them for something special?"

"So carpentry wasn't good enough for Mr. Big Shot?"

"Psst. Hey, mister, I got a message for your mayor. Tell him there's a plague of frogs camped just off Astoria in Queens. Tell him to cough up ten thousand gallons of flies or he won't even begin to know the meaning of the word trouble."

"My goodness, Grandmother . . . what an exceptionally
large clitoris you have!"

"Hey, John! Instead of giving you a haircut, this time I thought I'd just blow your fucking head off."

"We're going to have to prepare her Manhattan rather than New England style. She's having her period."

"It's your mother and she's covered with flies and shit. Should I let her in?"

"Snailman! Thank heavens!"

"Here we are, I'll put in your fifty cents. Okay, here we go. Oh boy, this looks like a real sizzler. It shows this girl on a bed with only panties on—wow! What a pair of knockers on her! A guy is walkin' over to her and he's unzipping his fly, now she starts takin' her panties off and he..."

"If you're ever sick or anything and your secretary needs some papers signed, I can do your signature perfectly."

"Let's faunicate."

"NONE OF THE GUYS DOWN AT THE HOME FOR THE BLIND WILL BELIEVE THAT I SLEPT WITH BO DEREK!"

"Ingemar has always marched to the beat of a different drummer."

"C'mon, Winky.... Bad enough it's a slow corner, but I'll never sell any pencils if you keep humping my leg!"

"Maybe he can't swim."

"Yes. I have a question. Will we
get a chance to fuck a horse?"

"…And we were able to survive the two and a half hours that we were stuck between the eighth and ninth floors by drinking our own urine."

E. SUBITZKY

"Hey, Dad, can I have the car tonight?"

S.GROSS

"*Second question: This is the first time I've ever gone down on a perfect stranger—true or false?*"

"*Hey, how about a vegetable?*"

"Of course, the original pendulum kept better time."

"*You know, I'd be out of business if it weren't for self-destructive perverted bastards like you.*"

"He followed me home, mom. Can I eat him?"

S. GROSS

"I am not a scale. I am a Martian.
You are standing on my testicles."

"*Well! I think this calls for a little drink.*"

"*Madam, I think one of the reasons you're not satisfied with your vibrator is that you expect too much from it.*"

"Did you see where I put my goddam nuts?"

"Not all of us are like this. I have a problem with premature ejaculation."

"Oh, wow, like where do you get your ideas?"

90

"No need to pay me, madam—I'll just sniff the monkey's finger."

"I guess we never should have gotten married, eh, sis?"

"Doctor, this is Mr. Gusset. Mr. Gusset thinks he's the Empire State Building."

"*Bless me, Father, for I have sinned....*"

"Say, buddy, you got any idea where
the Illiterate Club is?"

"I'm sorry, the parents of the young man in that wreck
refuse to donate his liver. They are, however, giving me
an excellent deal on parts for my Porsche."

"Which do you prefer—sharing a room with a person who's slightly out of his mind from heavy medication, or a room with a person who's throwing up all the time?"

"Be careful, dear, it might be poisonous."

"What if I was to give you a choice, Helen. . . . I can say I'm sorry for being insensitive to your needs and not taking your feelings about our relationship seriously, whereupon we make up and possibly even conclude the discussion with lovemaking. . . or I could just take a .357 magnum and paint the wall with your spoiled-little-white-bitch brains."

Carl Gets Up on the Wrong Side
of the Bed for the Last Time.

"My compliments to the chef!"

"Well, well, Heffernan! Associate editor at Harper's...
managing editor at the Atlantic...a nice stint with the
Times Book Review... May I say how pleased we are to have
you here at Oriental Wet Snatch Illustrated!"

"*I suppose this means we won't be able to go to school today?*"

"I'm doing one hell of a business with the S and M crowd."

"Al's a nice guy and everything, but never bone his wife, molest his children, and burn down his house all in the same day."

CALDWELL

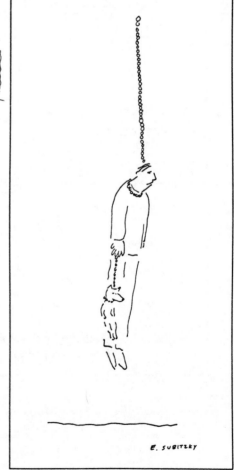

E. SUBITZKY

"*According to this there's nothing wrong with you . . . but then these are the papers to my house and car.*"

"The job doesn't pay very much, but I make it up to you by letting you sniff the seats."

"Where ya goin', wimp? A real man can <u>hold</u> his urine."

"No, I'm not expecting a child. On the contrary, I just ate one."

"No kidding—Stottlemeyer's date's got twelve tits."